Invitation to Love:

Living and Leading a Life of Overflow

From one man He made all the nations, that they should inhabit the whole earth;

and He marked out their appointed times in history and the boundaries of their lands.

God did this so that they would seek Him

and perhaps reach out for Him and find Him,

though He is not far from any one of us.

Acts 17:26-27

Karen Wycoff Watson

2017

OVERVIEW

Have you ever considered the entire Bible from cover to cover, Genesis to Revelation, is the story of God's love for mankind and His desire to be with us? Yes, it was written by many people. And yes, it consists of various books, letters, prayers, and stories that span the course of thousands of years. But it really is one story. It's the stunning saga of God's matchless, boundless, pursuing love for all of mankind and the great lengths He went to, to make a way for us, to be with Him.

We see in the beginning of the Bible, in Genesis, even after Adam and Eve chose not to believe God and ate what He warned them not to eat, He went to be with them. Genesis 3:9 says, *"But the LORD God called out to the man, "Where are you?""* Now Adam and Eve had gone into hiding as they felt shame when they noticed they were naked. But God knew all of this and went to them anyway. It goes on to say God went so far as to sew skins to cover their nakedness. Genesis 3:21 says, *"The LORD God made garments of skin for Adam and his wife and clothed them."* There is a lot we could talk about from all of this, but the point here is, God's desire was to be with His people right from the beginning and nothing could get in the way of that.

The other bookend of the Biblical account of God's desire to be with His people culminates in Revelation 21:2-4 which says,

"And I saw the holy city, the new Jerusalem,
coming down from God out of heaven like a bride beautifully dressed for her husband.

I heard a loud shout from the throne, saying, "Look, God's home is now among His people!

He will live with them, and they will be His people.

God Himself will be with them.

He will wipe every tear from their eyes,

and there will be no more death or sorrow or crying or pain.

All these things are gone forever."

The outcome God has in mind for us, is to be with Him forever. We were made to be in communion with Him. This has been His purpose and plan from the beginning. There are many places in scripture where we see the clues of His desire, His intent to be in relationship with mankind. But suffice it to say, we only need to look to the Name of Jesus, Immanuel, the Name that means God With Us. We see the heart of God in the Name of His Son, Jesus.

One of the central themes of this devotional Bible study is for us to really grasp God's desire for each of us, individually, to have an intimate, ongoing relationship with Him. Relationship with God Almighty! How amazing is that? The truth is, one of the aspects of God's very nature is He is eminently relational. We see this in what some refer to as the "dance of the Trinity." Father, Son, and Spirit, separate yet One, live eternally in joyful, generous, self-sustaining unity. They defer to and glorify One Another as they live in harmony and community. We see them together at Jesus' baptism when the Spirit came down and the Father said, *"You are My Son, Whom I love. With You I am well pleased."* There is also when Jesus was gloriously transfigured before Peter, John, and James on the mountainside. They actually heard the Father's voice say, *"This is My Son, Whom I have chosen; listen to Him."*

This *"listen to Him"* is an indication we, as followers of Christ, are invited into this community of love. The fact is, we are. God's nature is inclusionary. We were always meant to be in community with Him. We were always meant to dance!

It is interesting to note, as we study scripture, the many ways God is described which are clearly relational. Father, Bridegroom, Counselor, Master, High Priest, Friend, Teacher, Savior, Comforter, Lover, Shepherd, Guide, Strengthener, Redeemer, Immanuel (God with us). None of these words involve just one; they only work in relationship. We are the ones on the other side of these words of connection.

Paul's beautiful prayer in Ephesians 3:14-19 gives us a glimpse of how the Father, Son and Spirit work together in us.

When I think of all this, I fall to my knees and pray
to the Father, the Creator of everything in heaven and on earth.
I pray that from His glorious, unlimited resources He will empower you
with inner strength through His Spirit.
Then Christ will make His home in your hearts as you trust in Him.
Your roots will grow down into God's love and keep you strong.
And may you have the power to understand, as all God's people should,
how wide, how long, how high, and how deep His love is.
May you experience the love of Christ, though it is too great to understand fully.
Then you will be made complete
with all the fullness of life and power that comes from God.

Truth be told, we have a hard time imagining this kind of limitless love could actually be for us. Deep down we know we aren't exactly all that loveable, yet despite knowing this, we do so want to be loved. We need to be loved actually as we were made to be loved. Our souls seem to have an inkling of this as we all share an unquenchable thirst, an insatiable hunger, a yearning for love which is ever present whether we are conscious of it or not. The world offers myriads of ways men and women try to satisfy this desire within. And some of those things come close to satisfying us and are good. But how long do those things, those times last? Somehow we eventually learn the world offers nothing that completely provides what we crave.

The only way to find what we are ultimately looking for is when we turn to the one true God and allow His love to penetrate our souls. Paul tells us in Acts 17:26-27,

> *From one man He made all the nations,*
> *that they should inhabit the whole earth;*
> *and He marked out their appointed times in history*
> *and the boundaries of their lands.*
> *God did this so that they would seek Him*
> *and perhaps reach out for Him and find Him,*
> *though He is not far from any one of us.*

It is astonishing God is so close to us and that as we reach out for Him, we can find Him. We see David treasured the joy of knowing God's nearness and the intimacy of relationship with Him as we read his heartfelt prayer in Psalm 63.

God, You are my God; earnestly I seek You.

My soul thirsts for You; my whole being longs for You,

in a land parched and weary, without water.

I have seen You in the sanctuary and beheld Your power and Your glory.

Your unfailing love is better than life itself.

My lips praise you; all my life I will bless You. In Your Name I lift up my hands.

I will be fully satisfied as with the richest of foods.

On my lips is a song of joy and in my mouth, praise.

On my bed I think of You; I meditate on You all night long.

Because You are my help I sing for joy in the shadow of Your wings.

My soul clings to You. Your right hand supports me.

Only God's extravagant, never-ending love has the capability to satisfy our restless, fickle hearts. His love and His love alone, has the capacity to bring wholeness to our lives. The way we discover the love of God more and more is by seeking Him, day by day. We do this by reading the Bible, His revelation to us, as well as by praying, which is talking and listening to Him. Being in community with others who love the Lord is important as well. This is how we can encourage and be encouraged in our lives, as followers of Jesus Christ.

As we engage more and more, in this divine relationship we soon notice changes in our lives. We learn from Him and He begins to realign how we think and what we do. A desire takes root in our souls to want to do what is good and pleasing to Him. God's anointed inside-out life transformation begins to affect all areas of our lives. We come to know His loving Presence as a solid foundation we can build our lives on. Circumstances come and go but we discover His love is ever-present and unfailing. Somehow that changes everything. Our weary souls are refreshed and revived in the daily, ever-growing awareness of our loving God with us.

We would be remiss to not remember Jesus in the context of God's love. John tells us God Himself is love. He sent us His Son Jesus as the physical representation of His love. Jesus came to make a way for us to be in intimate relationship with God forever.

John tells us in John 3:16,

> For God so loved the world that He gave His one and only Son,
> that whoever believes in Him shall not perish but have eternal life.

He also says in I John 4:9-10,

> This is how God showed His love among us;
> He sent His one and only Son into the world that we might live through Him.
> This is love; not that we loved God
> but that He loved us and sent His Son as an atoning sacrifice for our sins.

Paul speaks to this in Romans 5:8,

> But God demonstrates His own love for us in this;
> while we were sinners, Christ died for us.

Jesus' life on earth was an observable demonstration of God's love. His was a tangible and extremely costly love. He not only came to us, He suffered and died for us. His life is the living illustration of what love lived out looks like.

We too can live lives of tangible love. As we are loved we are enabled to give love away. As early as in Genesis, we see what God gives to His people is never to be hoarded. In Genesis 12:1-2 God says to Abram,

"Leave your native country, your relatives, and your father's family,
and go to the land that I will show you. I will make you into a great nation.
I will bless you and make you famous, and you will be a blessing to others."

We are a people who are blessed to be a blessing, plain and simple. We see how God's people through the centuries, at times, forgot this. How sad it is we can easily forget as well.

The reality is we need to spend quality time with God so He can show us how He wants us to share His blessings with others in the context of our particular lives. Fueled and directed by God's Spirit we can show (not just talk about) love and grace to a broken and needy world. This is the life of overflow Jesus tells us about in John 15:9-13,

"I have loved you even as the Father has loved Me. Remain in My love.
When you obey My commandments, you remain in My love,
just as I obey My Father's commandments and remain in His love.
I have told you these things so that you will be filled with My joy.
Yes, your joy will overflow!
This is My commandment: Love each other in the same way I have loved you.
There is no greater love than to lay down one's life for one's friends.

Once we begin to "remain" in Jesus' love, we grow in our desire and ability to offer love to others. No strings attached. We begin to notice, not being perfectly loved by others is not of great concern to us because we are secure in the understanding of how deeply loved we are by God. Nothing can take His love away from us. As our identity is more and more firmly embedded in the soil of His love and grace, we are able reach out and offer love to those around us in concrete ways. This is the heart of *God's plan of living and leading the life of overflow* He wants us to live as His followers. He pours in and we pour out.

Paul talks of this overflow life in 2 Corinthians 5:14 when he says, *"Christ's loves compels us."* The love of God is the power source, which compels us, to express in deed and with our words, the good news of Jesus Christ. The Bible calls this expression of love, bearing fruit. The Lord gives us a great way to envision this in Jeremiah 17:7-8,

> *"But blessed is the one who trusts in the Lord, whose confidence is in Him.*
> *They will be like a tree planted by the water that sends out its roots by the stream.*
> *It does not fear when heat comes; its leaves are always green.*
> *It has no worries in a year of drought and never fails to bear fruit."*

This devotional Bible study is designed to help us consider deeply what God has done for us. We will see the nature of His love, how His love changes us (transforms us), and how it motivates us to love others (bears fruit through us). My prayer is there will be paradigm shifts within you as the Lord draws you ever closer. I pray you experience *changes within* as you grow in your awareness of God's grace towards you. External changes we (or others) try to impose upon ourselves in the name of religion are only effective for so long. But when we cooperate with the Holy Spirit's work within us He changes our hearts and our minds. His priorities and passions are formed in us. His character shapes ours more and more. This kind of life-giving change within, initiated by God, is always fruitful and lasting.

We can note these changes can come slowly, much to our dismay. Habits in how we think and behave are deeply ingrained within us. Thankfully God is patient with us as He works in our lives. We can see the process of spiritual maturing (which affects all areas of life) in the lives of many of our heroes in the Bible, Abraham, Moses, Joseph, David, Peter, Paul and many others, if we look for it. God changed them over the course of time, within the context of their lives. He used everything going on in and around them to grow them up, to become just whom He created them to be. Each of their journeys was unique just as ours are. So we are not alone in this life long process of spiritual transformation.

We can keep in mind none of their lives were failure or trouble free which is encouraging as it is the same with us. God is with us through the ups and downs of our lives, using it all to mature us in His ways (see Romans 8:28 and 29). The secret is to continue seeking Him no matter what challenges we face. It's actually most often during difficult times He shows us His mercy and grace as He teaches us great lessons for living. The prophet Isaiah gives us great promise of this in Isaiah 14:3, where he quotes the Lord saying, *"I will give you the treasures of darkness, riches stored in secret places so that you may know that I am the LORD, the God of Israel, who summons you by name."*

It is of my firm belief that consistent (not being rigid or legalistic about it) time spent with God in His Word (the Bible) is a crucial part of our life with Him. If we want to grow closer to the Lord, especially during times of trouble, time spent in the scriptures helps us develop a vibrant, intimate relationship with Him. He shows us Himself and ways of living that help guide our steps as we go. So this devotional Bible study's most important component is your time spent alone, in the passages of scripture provided, listening for what God might want to say to you. Hebrews 4:12 tells us God's Word (the Bible) is always relevant, personal, useful, and instructive for us. It helps us get to the heart of the matters that concern us and that concern God.

For the word of God is alive and active.
Sharper than any double-edged sword,
it penetrates even to dividing soul and spirit, joints and marrow;
it judges the thoughts and attitudes of the heart.

As you read the Bible, take stock of yourself. Don't worry about what state you're in. Who are we kidding when we think God doesn't already know, right? Come honestly before Him. Learn (and this can be a process) to trust what He says is always for your best.

Linger as you read. Don't read with the intent of merely gathering information *about God.* Think of this as reading relationally, as actually being in conversation *with God.* The Lord wants us to have an intimate knowing of Him, not just an intellectual knowing about Him. Stop and talk to the Lord as you read. Tell Him what's on your mind, your heart. Ask Him what's on His heart for you. This conversation is with the One Who knows you through and through, loves you, and always has the best in mind for you. It's not something to check off your to do list anymore than having a heart to heart conversation with a dear, trusted friend would be. This is a special time to spend one on One with your closest Friend. Whether this time is short or long it is always time well spent.

Ask the Holy Spirit to show you what He wants you to grasp as you read and pray. Take note of what you think He might be saying to you. You will soon notice, if you haven't already, He will show you what is relevant and applicable to what's going on in your life. It's quite remarkable. Also, keep in mind, just like as in any relationship, time and intentionality are how bonds are strengthened and trust is built.

In closing, I pray God's grace and peace are with you as discover more and more of the sheer magnitude of God's profound, personal, and intimate love *for you*. Here are the words I used to describe His love in this overview: matchless, boundless, pursuing, extravagant, never-ending, limitless, ever-present, unfailing, great, tangible, costly, profound, intimate, everlasting, immeasurable, and personal. Great superlatives! See if you can't add to this list, words you discover for yourself, of God's love towards you. I pray your life is filled to overflowing with God's joy as you seek Him day by day. And may He give you His power to share with the world around you, in big and little ways, His love and grace.

Enjoy the dance!

Karen Wycoff Watson
Carlsbad, California, 2017

May our Lord Jesus Christ Himself and God our Father, Who loved us
and by His grace gave us eternal encouragement and good hope,
encourage your hearts and strengthen you in every good deed and word.
2 Thessalonians 2:16-17

Getting Started

ଔ   You will find some passages of scripture lengthier than others. Being in the Word is never a "to do." It is a "being with." We read in relationship with God. So relax and enjoy your time with the Lord in His Word no matter how short or long your reading is. Go ahead and spread it out by doing as little or as much as you'd like on any given day.

ଔ   Read personally. Ask yourself and God how what you are reading relates to your (not everyone else's) life, right here and right now. How does it encourage you, instruct you, redirect you, warn you, give you hope, inform any decisions you need to make? Psalm 119:130 tells us,

"The unfolding of Your Words gives light; it gives understanding to the simple."
And then there is Psalm 119:105,

"Your Word is a lamp to guide my feet and a light for my path."

ଔ   Use this study as a journal. There is plenty of room for you to take notes as you read. Underline and circle things that stand out to you. Use the margins and space provided to journal, jot down questions, write insights and prayers, etc… as you go. This is a place to process what God is showing you.

ଔ   All passages of scripture you will look up are taken from the New Living Translation unless noted otherwise. You might want to find these passages in other translations to further enhance your understanding of any given passage.

ଔ   You can benefit by looking up the passages of scripture in your Bible to see the context of what comes before and after it. Context is always important.

ଔ   This study can be done on your own, at your own pace. If you do 5 passages a week and it is a 5-week study. Or you could spend a week in each passage. Find a rhythm that seems good for you and what is currently going on in your life.

ᘓ   Or you can do this study with a friend, again, at whatever pace suits your current seasons of life. It is great for a small group as well. If you do it with others, try to have everyone ponder and pray through the passages on their own before they come together for a discussion. Sharing what everyone discovers for himself or herself can be an insightful and rich time.

ᘓ   You might like to try different ways to interact with the passages of scriptures. One way would be to make a list of all you see as God's part in your relationship from the passage. Then make another list of what you see as your part. This really helps us see where we might be taking on what is not ours. It also builds awe and gratitude as we see just how much God does for us.

ᘓ   On the next pages are steps on how to use this devotional study. Please do your best to follow the steps. You will get the most from the scriptures by engaging in the process as suggested, including reading and rereading the passages.

Who has done such mighty deeds,
summoning each new generation from the beginning of time?
It is I, the Lord, the First and the Last.
I alone am He."
Isaiah 41:4

THE STEPS

⋐ STEP 1 ⋑

First take a few moments to ASK THE LORD to speak to you during this time with Him.

READ the passage slowly and prayerfully.

⋐ STEP 2 ⋑

READ it again, with this question in mind:

WHAT MIGHT THE LORD WANT ME TO NOTICE ABOUT HIM AS I READ?

Look for what you notice about the Lord. What can you learn about Him from what you are reading? From what He says, from what He does or doesn't do? What character qualities do you see in Him? What can you learn about His heart? How would you describe Him to someone who doesn't know Him from reading this passage of scripture? Journal your thoughts.

⋐ STEP 3 ⋑

READ once again and notice:

WHAT WORDS, PHRASES, PROMISES OR WARNINGS AM I DRAWN TO?

Don't over-think this. Just pay attention to a few words or phrases that resonate with you and jot them down. This isn't time to go into detail.

THE STEPS

ଓ STEP 4 ଥ

READ it again and ask yourself and God:

WHAT DO I THINK THE LORD IS SAYING TO ME, PERSONALLY,

AS I PRAYERFULLY LINGER IN HIS WORD TODAY?

How does what you are hearing from God intersect with what is currently going on in your life? God's Word speaks to us with relevance to our "right here, right now" lives. What do you sense God wants you to know from your time with Him today? Looking at the words or phrases you wrote down can help you with this. Is He encouraging you to act on anything specific or is it a reframing of an attitude? This could be something new to you or just a reminder.

ଓ STEP 5 ଥ

READ the passage one last time:

TAKE A FEW MOMENTS TO QUIET YOUR HEART AND THEN

WRITE AN HONEST PRAYER OF RESPONSE TO

WHAT YOU SENSE THE LORD IS SPEAKING INTO YOUR LIFE TODAY.

ଓ IN CONCLUSION ଥ

Ask the Lord to help you remember, as you go about your day, what He showed you from His Word. Let it encourage you in all you do. Remember, God works in us, not only for our own sake, but also for the sake of others. Ask Him to help you see opportunities to share His love today. This may or may not involve using words.

TABLE OF CONTENTS

TABLE OF CONTENTS

GOD'S INVITATION TO LOVE

Long ago the Lord said to Israel:
"I have loved you, My people, with an everlasting love.
With unfailing love I have drawn you to Myself.

Jeremiah 31:3

Isaiah 55:1-3

55:1 "Is anyone thirsty?

Come and drink—

even if you have no money!

Come, take your choice of wine or milk—

it's all free!

2 Why spend your money on food that does not give you strength?

Why pay for food that does you no good?

Listen to me, and you will eat what is good.

You will enjoy the finest food.

3 "Come to me with your ears wide open.

Listen, and you will find life.

I will make an everlasting covenant with you.

I will give you all the unfailing love I promised to David.

WHAT MIGHT THE LORD WANT ME TO NOTICE ABOUT HIM AS I READ?

WHAT WORDS, PHRASES, PROMISES OR WARNINGS AM I DRAWN TO?

WHAT DO I THINK THE LORD IS SAYING TO ME, PERSONALLY,

AS I PRAYERFULLY LINGER IN HIS WORD TODAY?

TAKE A FEW MOMENTS TO QUIET YOUR HEART AND THEN WRITE AN HONEST

PRAYER OF RESPONSE TO WHAT YOU SENSE THE LORD IS SPEAKING INTO YOUR

LIFE TODAY.

John 10:1-10

10:1 "I tell you the truth, anyone who sneaks over the wall of a sheepfold, rather than going through the gate, must surely be a thief and a robber! 2 But the one who enters through the gate is the shepherd of the sheep. 3 The gatekeeper opens the gate for him, and the sheep recognize his voice and come to him. He calls his own sheep by name and leads them out. 4 After he has gathered his own flock, he walks ahead of them, and they follow him because they know his voice. 5 They won't follow a stranger; they will run from him because they don't know his voice."

6 Those who heard Jesus use this illustration didn't understand what he meant, 7 so he explained it to them: "I tell you the truth, I am the gate for the sheep. 8 All who came before me were thieves and robbers. But the true sheep did not listen to them. 9 Yes, I am the gate. Those who come in through me will be saved. They will come and go freely and will find good pastures. 10 The thief's purpose is to steal and kill and destroy. My purpose is to give them a rich and satisfying life.

WHAT MIGHT THE LORD WANT ME TO NOTICE ABOUT HIM AS I READ?

WHAT WORDS, PHRASES, PROMISES OR WARNINGS AM I DRAWN TO?

WHAT DO I THINK THE LORD IS SAYING TO ME, PERSONALLY,

AS I PRAYERFULLY LINGER IN HIS WORD TODAY?

TAKE A FEW MOMENTS TO QUIET YOUR HEART AND THEN WRITE AN HONEST

PRAYER OF RESPONSE TO WHAT YOU SENSE THE LORD IS SPEAKING INTO YOUR

LIFE TODAY.

Matthew 11:25-30

11:25 At that time Jesus prayed this prayer: "O Father, Lord of heaven and earth, thank you for hiding these things from those who think themselves wise and clever, and for revealing them to the childlike.[26] Yes, Father, it pleased you to do it this way!

[27] "My Father has entrusted everything to me. No one truly knows the Son except the Father, and no one truly knows the Father except the Son and those to whom the Son chooses to reveal him."

[28] Then Jesus said, "Come to me, all of you who are weary and carry heavy burdens, and I will give you rest. [29] Take my yoke upon you. Let me teach you, because I am humble and gentle at heart, and you will find rest for your souls. [30] For my yoke is easy to bear, and the burden I give you is light."

Matthew 11:28-30 The Message

11:28 "Are you tired? Worn out? Burned out on religion? Come to me. Get away with me and you'll recover your life. I'll show you how to take a real rest. Walk with me and work with me— watch how I do it. Learn the unforced rhythms of grace. I won't lay anything heavy or ill-fitting on you. Keep company with me and you'll learn to live freely and lightly."

WHAT MIGHT THE LORD WANT ME TO NOTICE ABOUT HIM AS I READ?

WHAT WORDS, PHRASES, PROMISES OR WARNINGS AM I DRAWN TO?

WHAT DO I THINK THE LORD IS SAYING TO ME, PERSONALLY,

AS I PRAYERFULLY LINGER IN HIS WORD TODAY?

TAKE A FEW MOMENTS TO QUIET YOUR HEART AND THEN WRITE AN HONEST

PRAYER OF RESPONSE TO WHAT YOU SENSE THE LORD IS SPEAKING INTO YOUR

LIFE TODAY.

Ephesians 1:1-14

1:1 This letter is from Paul, chosen by the will of God to be an apostle of Christ Jesus.

I am writing to God's holy people in Ephesus, who are faithful followers of Christ Jesus.

2 May God our Father and the Lord Jesus Christ give you grace and peace.

3 All praise to God, the Father of our Lord Jesus Christ, who has blessed us with every spiritual blessing in the heavenly realms because we are united with Christ. 4 Even before he made the world, God loved us and chose us in Christ to be holy and without fault in his eyes. 5 God decided in advance to adopt us into his own family by bringing us to himself through Jesus Christ. This is what he wanted to do, and it gave him great pleasure. 6 So we praise God for the glorious grace he has poured out on us who belong to his dear Son. 7 He is so rich in kindness and grace that he purchased our freedom with the blood of his Son and forgave our sins. 8 He has showered his kindness on us, along with all wisdom and understanding.

9 God has now revealed to us his mysterious will regarding Christ—which is to fulfill his own good plan. 10 And this is the plan: At the right time he will bring everything together under the authority of Christ—everything in heaven and on earth. 11 Furthermore, because we are united with Christ, we have received an inheritance from God, for he chose us in advance, and he makes everything work out according to his plan.

12 God's purpose was that we Jews who were the first to trust in Christ would bring praise and glory to God. 13 And now you Gentiles have also heard the truth, the Good News that God saves you. And when you believed in Christ, he identified you as his own by giving you the Holy Spirit, whom he promised long ago. 14 The Spirit is God's guarantee that he will give us the inheritance he promised and that he has purchased us to be his own people. He did this so we would praise and glorify him.

WHAT MIGHT THE LORD WANT ME TO NOTICE ABOUT HIM AS I READ?

WHAT WORDS, PHRASES, PROMISES OR WARNINGS AM I DRAWN TO?

WHAT DO I THINK THE LORD IS SAYING TO ME, PERSONALLY,

AS I PRAYERFULLY LINGER IN HIS WORD TODAY?

TAKE A FEW MOMENTS TO QUIET YOUR HEART AND THEN WRITE AN HONEST

PRAYER OF RESPONSE TO WHAT YOU SENSE THE LORD IS SPEAKING INTO YOUR

LIFE TODAY.

Hebrews 4:14-16

4:14 So then, since we have a great High Priest who has entered heaven, Jesus the Son of God, let us hold firmly to what we believe. ¹⁵ This High Priest of ours understands our weaknesses, for he faced all of the same testings we do, yet he did not sin. ¹⁶ So let us come boldly to the throne of our gracious God. There we will receive his mercy, and we will find grace to help us when we need it most.

Hebrews 4:14-16 The Message

4:14 Now that we know what we have—Jesus, this great High Priest with ready access to God—let's not let it slip through our fingers. We don't have a priest who is out of touch with our reality. He's been through weakness and testing, experienced it all—all but the sin. So let's walk right up to him and get what he is so ready to give. Take the mercy, accept the help.

WHAT MIGHT THE LORD WANT ME TO NOTICE ABOUT HIM AS I READ?

WHAT WORDS, PHRASES, PROMISES OR WARNINGS AM I DRAWN TO?

WHAT DO I THINK THE LORD IS SAYING TO ME, PERSONALLY,

AS I PRAYERFULLY LINGER IN HIS WORD TODAY?

TAKE A FEW MOMENTS TO QUIET YOUR HEART AND THEN WRITE AN HONEST

PRAYER OF RESPONSE TO WHAT YOU SENSE THE LORD IS SPEAKING INTO YOUR

LIFE TODAY.

GOD'S STEADFAST LOVE

See how very much our Father loves us,

for He calls us His children, and that is what we are!

1 John 3:1

Psalm 23:1-6

23:1 The LORD is my shepherd;

   I have all that I need.

2 He lets me rest in green meadows;

   he leads me beside peaceful streams.

3   He renews my strength.

He guides me along right paths,

   bringing honor to his name.

4 Even when I walk

   through the darkest valley,

I will not be afraid,

   for you are close beside me.

Your rod and your staff

   protect and comfort me.

5 You prepare a feast for me

   in the presence of my enemies.

You honor me by anointing my head with oil.

   My cup overflows with blessings.

6 Surely your goodness and unfailing love will pursue me

   all the days of my life,

and I will live in the house of the LORD

   forever.

WHAT MIGHT THE LORD WANT ME TO NOTICE ABOUT HIM AS I READ?

WHAT WORDS, PHRASES, PROMISES OR WARNINGS AM I DRAWN TO?

WHAT DO I THINK THE LORD IS SAYING TO ME, PERSONALLY,

AS I PRAYERFULLY LINGER IN HIS WORD TODAY?

TAKE A FEW MOMENTS TO QUIET YOUR HEART AND THEN WRITE AN HONEST

PRAYER OF RESPONSE TO WHAT YOU SENSE THE LORD IS SPEAKING INTO YOUR

LIFE TODAY.

Psalm 36:5-9

36:5 Your unfailing love, O LORD, is as vast as the heavens;

your faithfulness reaches beyond the clouds.

6 Your righteousness is like the mighty mountains,

your justice like the ocean depths.

You care for people and animals alike, O LORD.

7 How precious is your unfailing love, O God!

All humanity finds shelter

in the shadow of your wings.

8 You feed them from the abundance of your own house,

letting them drink from your river of delights.

9 For you are the fountain of life,

the light by which we see.

WHAT MIGHT THE LORD WANT ME TO NOTICE ABOUT HIM AS I READ?

WHAT WORDS, PHRASES, PROMISES OR WARNINGS AM I DRAWN TO?

WHAT DO I THINK THE LORD IS SAYING TO ME, PERSONALLY,

AS I PRAYERFULLY LINGER IN HIS WORD TODAY?

TAKE A FEW MOMENTS TO QUIET YOUR HEART AND THEN WRITE AN HONEST

PRAYER OF RESPONSE TO WHAT YOU SENSE THE LORD IS SPEAKING INTO YOUR

LIFE TODAY.

John 3:16-17

3:16 "For this is how God loved the world: He gave his one and only Son, so that everyone who believes in him will not perish but have eternal life. [17] God sent his Son into the world not to judge the world, but to save the world through him.

1 John 4:9-10

4:9 God showed how much he loved us by sending his one and only Son into the world so that we might have eternal life through him. [10] This is real love—not that we loved God, but that he loved us and sent his Son as a sacrifice to take away our sins.

WHAT MIGHT THE LORD WANT ME TO NOTICE ABOUT HIM AS I READ?

WHAT WORDS, PHRASES, PROMISES OR WARNINGS AM I DRAWN TO?

WHAT DO I THINK THE LORD IS SAYING TO ME, PERSONALLY,

AS I PRAYERFULLY LINGER IN HIS WORD TODAY?

TAKE A FEW MOMENTS TO QUIET YOUR HEART AND THEN WRITE AN HONEST

PRAYER OF RESPONSE TO WHAT YOU SENSE THE LORD IS SPEAKING INTO YOUR

LIFE TODAY.

8:28 And we know that God causes everything to work together for the good of those who love God and are called according to his purpose for them. [29] For God knew his people in advance, and he chose them to become like his Son, so that his Son would be the firstborn among many brothers and sisters. [30] And having chosen them, he called them to come to him. And having called them, he gave them right standing with himself. And having given them right standing, he gave them his glory.

[31] What shall we say about such wonderful things as these? If God is for us, who can ever be against us? [32] Since he did not spare even his own Son but gave him up for us all, won't he also give us everything else? [33] Who dares accuse us whom God has chosen for his own? No one—for God himself has given us right standing with himself. [34] Who then will condemn us? No one—for Christ Jesus died for us and was raised to life for us, and he is sitting in the place of honor at God's right hand, pleading for us.

[35] Can anything ever separate us from Christ's love? Does it mean he no longer loves us if we have trouble or calamity, or are persecuted, or hungry, or destitute, or in danger, or threatened with death? [36] (As the Scriptures say, "For your sake we are killed every day; we are being slaughtered like sheep.") [37] No, despite all these things, overwhelming victory is ours through Christ, who loved us.

[38] And I am convinced that nothing can ever separate us from God's love. Neither death nor life, neither angels nor demons, neither our fears for today nor our worries about tomorrow—not even the powers of hell can separate us from God's love. [39] No power in the sky above or in the earth below—indeed, nothing in all creation will ever be able to separate us from the love of God that is revealed in Christ Jesus our Lord.

WHAT MIGHT THE LORD WANT ME TO NOTICE ABOUT HIM AS I READ?

WHAT WORDS, PHRASES, PROMISES OR WARNINGS AM I DRAWN TO?

WHAT DO I THINK THE LORD IS SAYING TO ME, PERSONALLY,

AS I PRAYERFULLY LINGER IN HIS WORD TODAY?

TAKE A FEW MOMENTS TO QUIET YOUR HEART AND THEN WRITE AN HONEST

PRAYER OF RESPONSE TO WHAT YOU SENSE THE LORD IS SPEAKING INTO YOUR

LIFE TODAY.

1 Corinthians 13:4-8 & 14:1a

13:4 Love is patient and kind. Love is not jealous or boastful or proud [5] or rude. It does not demand its own way. It is not irritable, and it keeps no record of being wronged. [6] It does not rejoice about injustice but rejoices whenever the truth wins out. [7] Love never gives up, never loses faith, is always hopeful, and endures through every circumstance. 8 Love never fails [it never fades nor ends].

14:1 Let love be your highest goal!

1 Corinthians 13:4-8 & 14:1a The Amplified Version

13:4 Love endures with patience *and* serenity, love is kind *and* thoughtful, and is not jealous *or* envious; love does not brag and is not proud *or* arrogant. 5 It is not rude; it is not self-seeking, it is not provoked [nor overly sensitive and easily angered]; it does not take into account a wrong *endured*. 6 It does not rejoice at injustice, but rejoices with the truth [when right and truth prevail]. 7 Love bears all things [regardless of what comes], believes all things [looking for the best in each one], hopes all things [remaining steadfast during difficult times], endures all things [without weakening]. 8 Love never fails [it never fades nor ends].

14:1 Pursue [this] love [with eagerness, make it your goal].

WHAT MIGHT THE LORD WANT ME TO NOTICE ABOUT HIM AS I READ?

WHAT WORDS, PHRASES, PROMISES OR WARNINGS AM I DRAWN TO?

WHAT DO I THINK THE LORD IS SAYING TO ME, PERSONALLY,

AS I PRAYERFULLY LINGER IN HIS WORD TODAY?

TAKE A FEW MOMENTS TO QUIET YOUR HEART AND THEN WRITE AN HONEST

PRAYER OF RESPONSE TO WHAT YOU SENSE THE LORD IS SPEAKING INTO YOUR

LIFE TODAY.

THE LIFE TRANSFORMING NATURE OF GOD'S LOVE

Now may the God of peace—who brought up from the dead our Lord Jesus,
the great Shepherd of the sheep, and ratified an eternal covenant with His blood—
may He equip you with all you need for doing His will.
May He produce in you, through the power of Jesus Christ,
every good thing that is pleasing to Him.
All glory to Him forever and ever! Amen.

Hebrews 13:20-21

2 Corinthians 3:16-18

3:16 But whenever someone turns to the Lord, the veil is taken away.[17] For the Lord is the Spirit, and wherever the Spirit of the Lord is, there is freedom. [18] So all of us who have had that veil removed can see and reflect the glory of the Lord. And the Lord—who is the Spirit—makes us more and more like him as we are changed into his glorious image.

2 Corinthians 3:16-18 The Message

3:16 Whenever, though, they turn to face God as Moses did, God removes the veil and there they are—face-to-face! They suddenly recognize that God is a living, personal presence, not a piece of chiseled stone. And when God is personally present, a living Spirit, that old, constricting legislation is recognized as obsolete. We're free of it! All of us! Nothing between us and God, our faces shining with the brightness of his face. And so we are transfigured much like the Messiah, our lives gradually becoming brighter and more beautiful as God enters our lives and we become like him.

WHAT MIGHT THE LORD WANT ME TO NOTICE ABOUT HIM AS I READ?

WHAT WORDS, PHRASES, PROMISES OR WARNINGS AM I DRAWN TO?

WHAT DO I THINK THE LORD IS SAYING TO ME, PERSONALLY,

AS I PRAYERFULLY LINGER IN HIS WORD TODAY?

TAKE A FEW MOMENTS TO QUIET YOUR HEART AND THEN WRITE AN HONEST

PRAYER OF RESPONSE TO WHAT YOU SENSE THE LORD IS SPEAKING INTO YOUR

LIFE TODAY.

Romans 12:1-2

12:1 And so, dear brothers and sisters, I plead with you to give your bodies to God because of all he has done for you. Let them be a living and holy sacrifice—the kind he will find acceptable. This is truly the way to worship him. [2] Don't copy the behavior and customs of this world, but let God transform you into a new person by changing the way you think. Then you will learn to know God's will for you, which is good and pleasing and perfect.

Romans 12:1-2 The Message

12:1 So here's what I want you to do, God helping you: Take your everyday, ordinary life—your sleeping, eating, going-to-work, and walking-around life—and place it before God as an offering. Embracing what God does for you is the best thing you can do for him. Don't become so well-adjusted to your culture that you fit into it without even thinking. Instead, fix your attention on God. You'll be changed from the inside out. Readily recognize what he wants from you, and quickly respond to it. Unlike the culture around you, always dragging you down to its level of immaturity, God brings the best out of you, develops well-formed maturity in you.

WHAT MIGHT THE LORD WANT ME TO NOTICE ABOUT HIM AS I READ?

WHAT WORDS, PHRASES, PROMISES OR WARNINGS AM I DRAWN TO?

WHAT DO I THINK THE LORD IS SAYING TO ME, PERSONALLY,

AS I PRAYERFULLY LINGER IN HIS WORD TODAY?

TAKE A FEW MOMENTS TO QUIET YOUR HEART AND THEN WRITE AN HONEST

PRAYER OF RESPONSE TO WHAT YOU SENSE THE LORD IS SPEAKING INTO YOUR

LIFE TODAY.

5:16 So I say, let the Holy Spirit guide your lives. Then you won't be doing what your sinful nature craves. 17 The sinful nature wants to do evil, which is just the opposite of what the Spirit wants. And the Spirit gives us desires that are the opposite of what the sinful nature desires. These two forces are constantly fighting each other, so you are not free to carry out your good intentions. 18 But when you are directed by the Spirit, you are not under obligation to the law of Moses.

19 When you follow the desires of your sinful nature, the results are very clear: sexual immorality, impurity, lustful pleasures, 20 idolatry, sorcery, hostility, quarreling, jealousy, outbursts of anger, selfish ambition, dissension, division, 21 envy, drunkenness, wild parties, and other sins like these. Let me tell you again, as I have before, that anyone living that sort of life will not inherit the Kingdom of God.

22 But the Holy Spirit produces this kind of fruit in our lives: love, joy, peace, patience, kindness, goodness, faithfulness, 23 gentleness, and self-control. There is no law against these things!

24 Those who belong to Christ Jesus have nailed the passions and desires of their sinful nature to his cross and crucified them there. 25 Since we are living by the Spirit, let us follow the Spirit's leading in every part of our lives. 26 Let us not become conceited, or provoke one another, or be jealous of one another.

WHAT MIGHT THE LORD WANT ME TO NOTICE ABOUT HIM AS I READ?

WHAT WORDS, PHRASES, PROMISES OR WARNINGS AM I DRAWN TO?

WHAT DO I THINK THE LORD IS SAYING TO ME, PERSONALLY,

AS I PRAYERFULLY LINGER IN HIS WORD TODAY?

TAKE A FEW MOMENTS TO QUIET YOUR HEART AND THEN WRITE AN HONEST

PRAYER OF RESPONSE TO WHAT YOU SENSE THE LORD IS SPEAKING INTO YOUR

LIFE TODAY.

Ephesians 3:14-21

3:14 When I think of all this, I fall to my knees and pray to the Father, [15] the Creator of everything in heaven and on earth. [16] I pray that from his glorious, unlimited resources he will empower you with inner strength through his Spirit. [17] Then Christ will make his home in your hearts as you trust in him. Your roots will grow down into God's love and keep you strong. [18] And may you have the power to understand, as all God's people should, how wide, how long, how high, and how deep his love is. [19] May you experience the love of Christ, though it is too great to understand fully. Then you will be made complete with all the fullness of life and power that comes from God.

[20] Now all glory to God, who is able, through his mighty power at work within us, to accomplish infinitely more than we might ask or think. [21] Glory to him in the church and in Christ Jesus through all generations forever and ever! Amen.

Ephesians 3:14-21 The Message

3:14 My response is to get down on my knees before the Father, this magnificent Father who parcels out all heaven and earth. I ask him to strengthen you by his Spirit—not a brute strength but a glorious inner strength—that Christ will live in you as you open the door and invite him in. And I ask him that with both feet planted firmly on love, you'll be able to take in with all followers of Jesus the extravagant dimensions of Christ's love. Reach out and experience the breadth! Test its length! Plumb the depths! Rise to the heights! Live full lives, full in the fullness of God. God can do anything, you know—far more than you could ever imagine or guess or request in your wildest dreams! He does it not by pushing us around but by working within us, his Spirit deeply and gently within us.

Glory to God in the church! Glory to God in the Messiah, in Jesus!

Glory down all the generations! Glory through all millennia! Oh, yes!

WHAT MIGHT THE LORD WANT ME TO NOTICE ABOUT HIM AS I READ?

WHAT WORDS, PHRASES, PROMISES OR WARNINGS AM I DRAWN TO?

WHAT DO I THINK THE LORD IS SAYING TO ME, PERSONALLY,

AS I PRAYERFULLY LINGER IN HIS WORD TODAY?

TAKE A FEW MOMENTS TO QUIET YOUR HEART AND THEN WRITE AN HONEST

PRAYER OF RESPONSE TO WHAT YOU SENSE THE LORD IS SPEAKING INTO YOUR

LIFE TODAY.

Philippians 1:1-11

1:1 This letter is from Paul and Timothy, slaves of Christ Jesus.

I am writing to all of God's holy people in Philippi who belong to Christ Jesus, including the church leaders and deacons.

2 May God our Father and the Lord Jesus Christ give you grace and peace.

3 Every time I think of you, I give thanks to my God. 4 Whenever I pray, I make my requests for all of you with joy, 5 for you have been my partners in spreading the Good News about Christ from the time you first heard it until now. 6 And I am certain that God, who began the good work within you, will continue his work until it is finally finished on the day when Christ Jesus returns.

7 So it is right that I should feel as I do about all of you, for you have a special place in my heart. You share with me the special favor of God, both in my imprisonment and in defending and confirming the truth of the Good News. 8 God knows how much I love you and long for you with the tender compassion of Christ Jesus.

9 I pray that your love will overflow more and more, and that you will keep on growing in knowledge and understanding. 10 For I want you to understand what really matters, so that you may live pure and blameless lives until the day of Christ's return. 11 May you always be filled with the fruit of your salvation—the righteous character produced in your life by Jesus Christ—for this will bring much glory and praise to God.

WHAT MIGHT THE LORD WANT ME TO NOTICE ABOUT HIM AS I READ?

WHAT WORDS, PHRASES, PROMISES OR WARNINGS AM I DRAWN TO?

WHAT DO I THINK THE LORD IS SAYING TO ME, PERSONALLY,

AS I PRAYERFULLY LINGER IN HIS WORD TODAY?

TAKE A FEW MOMENTS TO QUIET YOUR HEART AND THEN WRITE AN HONEST

PRAYER OF RESPONSE TO WHAT YOU SENSE THE LORD IS SPEAKING INTO YOUR

LIFE TODAY.

GOD'S LOVE OVERFLOWING —

BEGRING FRUIT

And may the Lord make your love for one another

and for all people grow and overflow,

just as our love for you overflows.

1 Thessalonians 3:12

Psalm 1:1-3

1:1 Oh, the joys of those who do not

follow the advice of the wicked,

or stand around with sinners,

or join in with mockers.

2 But they delight in the law of the LORD,

meditating on it day and night.

3 They are like trees planted along the riverbank,

bearing fruit each season.

Their leaves never wither,

and they prosper in all they do.

Jeremiah 17:7-8

17:7 But blessed are those who trust in the LORD

and have made the LORD their hope and confidence.

8 They are like trees planted along a riverbank,

with roots that reach deep into the water.

Such trees are not bothered by the heat

or worried by long months of drought.

Their leaves stay green,

and they never stop producing fruit.

WHAT MIGHT THE LORD WANT ME TO NOTICE ABOUT HIM AS I READ?

WHAT WORDS, PHRASES, PROMISES OR WARNINGS AM I DRAWN TO?

WHAT DO I THINK THE LORD IS SAYING TO ME, PERSONALLY,

AS I PRAYERFULLY LINGER IN HIS WORD TODAY?

TAKE A FEW MOMENTS TO QUIET YOUR HEART AND THEN WRITE AN HONEST

PRAYER OF RESPONSE TO WHAT YOU SENSE THE LORD IS SPEAKING INTO YOUR

LIFE TODAY.

John 15:1-17

15:1 "I am the true grapevine, and my Father is the gardener. ² He cuts off every branch of mine that doesn't produce fruit, and he prunes the branches that do bear fruit so they will produce even more. ³ You have already been pruned and purified by the message I have given you.⁴ Remain in me, and I will remain in you. For a branch cannot produce fruit if it is severed from the vine, and you cannot be fruitful unless you remain in me.

⁵ "Yes, I am the vine; you are the branches. Those who remain in me, and I in them, will produce much fruit. For apart from me you can do nothing. ⁶ Anyone who does not remain in me is thrown away like a useless branch and withers. Such branches are gathered into a pile to be burned. ⁷ But if you remain in me and my words remain in you, you may ask for anything you want, and it will be granted! ⁸ When you produce much fruit, you are my true disciples. This brings great glory to my Father.

⁹ "I have loved you even as the Father has loved me. Remain in my love. ¹⁰ When you obey my commandments, you remain in my love, just as I obey my Father's commandments and remain in his love. ¹¹ I have told you these things so that you will be filled with my joy. Yes, your joy will overflow! ¹² This is my commandment: Love each other in the same way I have loved you. ¹³ There is no greater love than to lay down one's life for one's friends. ¹⁴ You are my friends if you do what I command. ¹⁵ I no longer call you slaves, because a master doesn't confide in his slaves. Now you are my friends, since I have told you everything the Father told me. ¹⁶ You didn't choose me. I chose you. I appointed you to go and produce lasting fruit, so that the Father will give you whatever you ask for, using my name. ¹⁷ This is my command: Love each other.

WHAT MIGHT THE LORD WANT ME TO NOTICE ABOUT HIM AS I READ?

WHAT WORDS, PHRASES, PROMISES OR WARNINGS AM I DRAWN TO?

WHAT DO I THINK THE LORD IS SAYING TO ME, PERSONALLY,

AS I PRAYERFULLY LINGER IN HIS WORD TODAY?

TAKE A FEW MOMENTS TO QUIET YOUR HEART AND THEN WRITE AN HONEST

PRAYER OF RESPONSE TO WHAT YOU SENSE THE LORD IS SPEAKING INTO YOUR

LIFE TODAY.

Ephesians 2:4-10

2:4 But God is so rich in mercy, and he loved us so much, 5 that even though we were dead because of our sins, he gave us life when he raised Christ from the dead. (It is only by God's grace that you have been saved!) 6 For he raised us from the dead along with Christ and seated us with him in the heavenly realms because we are united with Christ Jesus. 7 So God can point to us in all future ages as examples of the incredible wealth of his grace and kindness toward us, as shown in all he has done for us who are united with Christ Jesus.

8 God saved you by his grace when you believed. And you can't take credit for this; it is a gift from God. 9 Salvation is not a reward for the good things we have done, so none of us can boast about it. 10 For we are God's masterpiece. He has created us anew in Christ Jesus, so we can do the good things he planned for us long ago.

WHAT MIGHT THE LORD WANT ME TO NOTICE ABOUT HIM AS I READ?

WHAT WORDS, PHRASES, PROMISES OR WARNINGS AM I DRAWN TO?

WHAT DO I THINK THE LORD IS SAYING TO ME, PERSONALLY,

AS I PRAYERFULLY LINGER IN HIS WORD TODAY?

TAKE A FEW MOMENTS TO QUIET YOUR HEART AND THEN WRITE AN HONEST

PRAYER OF RESPONSE TO WHAT YOU SENSE THE LORD IS SPEAKING INTO YOUR

LIFE TODAY.

1:2 We are writing to God's holy people in the city of Colosse, who are faithful brothers and sisters in Christ. May God our Father give you grace and peace.

3 We always pray for you, and we give thanks to God, the Father of our Lord Jesus Christ. 4 For we have heard of your faith in Christ Jesus and your love for all of God's people, 5 which come from your confident hope of what God has reserved for you in heaven. You have had this expectation ever since you first heard the truth of the Good News.

6 This same Good News that came to you is going out all over the world. It is bearing fruit everywhere by changing lives, just as it changed your lives from the day you first heard and understood the truth about God's wonderful grace.

7 You learned about the Good News from Epaphras, our beloved co-worker. He is Christ's faithful servant, and he is helping us on your behalf. 8 He has told us about the love for others that the Holy Spirit has given you.

9 So we have not stopped praying for you since we first heard about you. We ask God to give you complete knowledge of his will and to give you spiritual wisdom and understanding. 10 Then the way you live will always honor and please the Lord, and your lives will produce every kind of good fruit. All the while, you will grow as you learn to know God better and better.

11 We also pray that you will be strengthened with all his glorious power so you will have all the endurance and patience you need. May you be filled with joy, 12 always thanking the Father. He has enabled you to share in the inheritance that belongs to his people, who live in the light. 13 For he has rescued us from the kingdom of darkness and transferred us into the Kingdom of his dear Son, 14 who purchased our freedom and forgave our sins.

WHAT MIGHT THE LORD WANT ME TO NOTICE ABOUT HIM AS I READ?

WHAT WORDS, PHRASES, PROMISES OR WARNINGS AM I DRAWN TO?

WHAT DO I THINK THE LORD IS SAYING TO ME, PERSONALLY,
AS I PRAYERFULLY LINGER IN HIS WORD TODAY?

TAKE A FEW MOMENTS TO QUIET YOUR HEART AND THEN WRITE AN HONEST
PRAYER OF RESPONSE TO WHAT YOU SENSE THE LORD IS SPEAKING INTO YOUR
LIFE TODAY.

1:2 May God give you more and more grace and peace as you grow in your knowledge of God and Jesus our Lord.

3 By his divine power, God has given us everything we need for living a godly life. We have received all of this by coming to know him, the one who called us to himself by means of his marvelous glory and excellence. 4 And because of his glory and excellence, he has given us great and precious promises. These are the promises that enable you to share his divine nature and escape the world's corruption caused by human desires.

5 In view of all this, make every effort to respond to God's promises. Supplement your faith with a generous provision of moral excellence, and moral excellence with knowledge, 6 and knowledge with self-control, and self-control with patient endurance, and patient endurance with godliness, 7 and godliness with brotherly affection, and brotherly affection with love for everyone.

8 The more you grow like this, the more productive and useful you will be in your knowledge of our Lord Jesus Christ.

WHAT MIGHT THE LORD WANT ME TO NOTICE ABOUT HIM AS I READ?

WHAT WORDS, PHRASES, PROMISES OR WARNINGS AM I DRAWN TO?

WHAT DO I THINK THE LORD IS SAYING TO ME, PERSONALLY,

AS I PRAYERFULLY LINGER IN HIS WORD TODAY?

TAKE A FEW MOMENTS TO QUIET YOUR HEART AND THEN WRITE AN HONEST
PRAYER OF RESPONSE TO WHAT YOU SENSE THE LORD IS SPEAKING INTO YOUR
LIFE TODAY.

GOD'S LOVING PRESENCE
WITH US ~ always

Those who trust in the Lord are as secure as Mount Zion;
they will not be defeated but will endure forever.
Just as the mountains surround Jerusalem,
so the Lord surrounds His people, both now and forever.

Psalm 125:2

Deuteronomy 31:6-8

31:6 So be strong and courageous! Do not be afraid and do not panic before them. For the LORD your God will personally go ahead of you. He will neither fail you nor abandon you."

7 Then Moses called for Joshua, and as all Israel watched, he said to him, "Be strong and courageous! For you will lead these people into the land that the LORD swore to their ancestors he would give them. You are the one who will divide it among them as their grants of land. 8 Do not be afraid or discouraged, for the LORD will personally go ahead of you. He will be with you; he will neither fail you nor abandon you."

Joshua 1:7-9

1:7 Be strong and very courageous. Be careful to obey all the instructions Moses gave you. Do not deviate from them, turning either to the right or to the left. Then you will be successful in everything you do. 8 Study this Book of Instruction continually. Meditate on it day and night so you will be sure to obey everything written in it. Only then will you prosper and succeed in all you do. 9 This is my command—be strong and courageous! Do not be afraid or discouraged. For the Lord your God is with you wherever you go."

WHAT MIGHT THE LORD WANT ME TO NOTICE ABOUT HIM AS I READ?

WHAT WORDS, PHRASES, PROMISES OR WARNINGS AM I DRAWN TO?

WHAT DO I THINK THE LORD IS SAYING TO ME, PERSONALLY,

AS I PRAYERFULLY LINGER IN HIS WORD TODAY?

TAKE A FEW MOMENTS TO QUIET YOUR HEART AND THEN WRITE AN HONEST

PRAYER OF RESPONSE TO WHAT YOU SENSE THE LORD IS SPEAKING INTO YOUR

LIFE TODAY.

Psalm 139:1-18

139:1 LORD, you have examined my heart and know everything about me.

2 You know when I sit down or stand up. You know my thoughts even when I'm far away.

3 You see me when I travel and when I rest at home. You know everything I do.

4 You know what I am going to say even before I say it, LORD.

5 You go before me and follow me. You place your hand of blessing on my head.

6 Such knowledge is too wonderful for me, too great for me to understand!

7 I can never escape from your Spirit! I can never get away from your presence!

8 If I go up to heaven, you are there; if I go down to the grave, you are there.

9 If I ride the wings of the morning, if I dwell by the farthest oceans,

10 even there your hand will guide me, and your strength will support me.

11 I could ask the darkness to hide me and the light around me to become night—

12 but even in darkness I cannot hide from you. To you the night shines as bright as day.

   Darkness and light are the same to you.

13 You made all the delicate, inner parts of my body and knit me together in my mother's womb.

14 Thank you for making me so wonderfully complex! Your workmanship is marvelous—how well I know it.

15 You watched me as I was being formed in utter seclusion, as I was woven together in the dark of the womb.

16 You saw me before I was born. Every day of my life was recorded in your book. Every moment was laid out before a single day had passed.

17 How precious are your thoughts about me, O God. They cannot be numbered!

18 I can't even count them; they outnumber the grains of sand! And when I wake up,

   you are still with me!

WHAT MIGHT THE LORD WANT ME TO NOTICE ABOUT HIM AS I READ?

WHAT WORDS, PHRASES, PROMISES OR WARNINGS AM I DRAWN TO?

WHAT DO I THINK THE LORD IS SAYING TO ME, PERSONALLY,

AS I PRAYERFULLY LINGER IN HIS WORD TODAY?

TAKE A FEW MOMENTS TO QUIET YOUR HEART AND THEN WRITE AN HONEST

PRAYER OF RESPONSE TO WHAT YOU SENSE THE LORD IS SPEAKING INTO YOUR

LIFE TODAY.

Isaiah 43:1-5

43:1 But now, O Jacob, listen to the Lord who created you.

O Israel, the one who formed you says,

"Do not be afraid, for I have ransomed you.

I have called you by name; you are mine.

2 When you go through deep waters,

I will be with you.

When you go through rivers of difficulty,

you will not drown.

When you walk through the fire of oppression,

you will not be burned up;

the flames will not consume you.

3 For I am the Lord, your God,

the Holy One of Israel, your Savior.

I gave Egypt as a ransom for your freedom;

I gave Ethiopia and Seba in your place.

4 Others were given in exchange for you.

I traded their lives for yours

because you are precious to me.

You are honored, and I love you.

5 "Do not be afraid, for I am with you.

I will gather you and your children from east and west.

WHAT MIGHT THE LORD WANT ME TO NOTICE ABOUT HIM AS I READ?

WHAT WORDS, PHRASES, PROMISES OR WARNINGS AM I DRAWN TO?

WHAT DO I THINK THE LORD IS SAYING TO ME, PERSONALLY,

AS I PRAYERFULLY LINGER IN HIS WORD TODAY?

TAKE A FEW MOMENTS TO QUIET YOUR HEART AND THEN WRITE AN HONEST

PRAYER OF RESPONSE TO WHAT YOU SENSE THE LORD IS SPEAKING INTO YOUR

LIFE TODAY.

Zephaniah 3:14-17

3:14 Sing, O daughter of Zion;

   shout aloud, O Israel!

Be glad and rejoice with all your heart,

   O daughter of Jerusalem!

15 For the LORD will remove his hand of judgment

   and will disperse the armies of your enemy.

And the LORD himself, the King of Israel,

   will live among you!

At last your troubles will be over,

   and you will never again fear disaster.

16 On that day the announcement to Jerusalem will be,

   "Cheer up, Zion! Don't be afraid!

17 For the LORD your God is living among you.

   He is a mighty savior.

He will take delight in you with gladness.

   With his love, he will calm all your fears.

   He will rejoice over you with joyful songs."

WHAT MIGHT THE LORD WANT ME TO NOTICE ABOUT HIM AS I READ?

WHAT WORDS, PHRASES, PROMISES OR WARNINGS AM I DRAWN TO?

WHAT DO I THINK THE LORD IS SAYING TO ME, PERSONALLY,

AS I PRAYERFULLY LINGER IN HIS WORD TODAY?

TAKE A FEW MOMENTS TO QUIET YOUR HEART AND THEN WRITE AN HONEST

PRAYER OF RESPONSE TO WHAT YOU SENSE THE LORD IS SPEAKING INTO YOUR

LIFE TODAY.

Matthew 28:16-20

28:16 Then the eleven disciples left for Galilee, going to the mountain where Jesus had told them to go. 17 When they saw him, they worshiped him—but some of them doubted! 18 Jesus came and told his disciples, "I have been given all authority in heaven and on earth. 19 Therefore, go and make disciples of all the nations, baptizing them in the name of the Father and the Son and the Holy Spirit. 20 Teach these new disciples to obey all the commands I have given you. And be sure of this: I am with you always, even to the end of the age."

Matthew 28:16-20 The Message

28:16 Meanwhile, the eleven disciples were on their way to Galilee, headed for the mountain Jesus had set for their reunion. The moment they saw him they worshiped him. Some, though, held back, not sure about worship, about risking themselves totally.

Jesus, undeterred, went right ahead and gave his charge: "God authorized and commanded me to commission you: Go out and train everyone you meet, far and near, in this way of life, marking them by baptism in the threefold name: Father, Son, and Holy Spirit. Then instruct them in the practice of all I have commanded you. I'll be with you as you do this, day after day after day, right up to the end of the age."

WHAT MIGHT THE LORD WANT ME TO NOTICE ABOUT HIM AS I READ?

WHAT WORDS, PHRASES, PROMISES OR WARNINGS AM I DRAWN TO?

WHAT DO I THINK THE LORD IS SAYING TO ME, PERSONALLY,

AS I PRAYERFULLY LINGER IN HIS WORD TODAY?

TAKE A FEW MOMENTS TO QUIET YOUR HEART AND THEN WRITE AN HONEST

PRAYER OF RESPONSE TO WHAT YOU SENSE THE LORD IS SPEAKING INTO YOUR

LIFE TODAY.

Made in the USA
Middletown, DE
11 April 2022